✓CL

D0821078

2x 6/09 8/09

AUG -- 2006

2006

Fact Finders™

Biographies

Sojourner Truth

Freedom Fighter

by Katherine Krohn

Consultant:
Dr. Kenneth Goings, Professor and Chair
Department of African American and African Studies
The Ohio State University
Columbus, Ohio

SAN DIEGO PUBLIC LIBRARY
CLAIREMONT

Capstone
press

Mankato, Minnesota

3 1336 07260 2015

Fact Finders is published by Capstone Press,
151 Good Counsel Drive, P.O. Box 669, Mankato, Minnesota 56002.
www.capstonepress.com

Copyright © 2006 by Capstone Press. All rights reserved.
No part of this publication may be reproduced in whole or in part, or stored in a retrieval
system, or transmitted in any form or by any means, electronic, mechanical, photocopying,
recording, or otherwise, without written permission of the publisher.
For information regarding permission, write to Capstone Press,
151 Good Counsel Drive, P.O. Box 669, Dept. R, Mankato, Minnesota 56002.
Printed in the United States of America

Library of Congress Cataloging-in-Publication Data
Krohn, Katherine E.
    Sojourner Truth: Freedom Fighter / by Katherine Krohn.
    p. cm.—(Fact finders. Biographies)
    Includes bibliographical references and index.
    ISBN 0-7368-4348-5 (hardcover)
    1. Truth, Sojourner, d. 1883—Juvenile literature. 2. African American abolitionists—
Biography—Juvenile literature. 3. African American women—Biography—Juvenile
literature. 4. Abolitionists—United States—Biography—Juvenile literature. 5. Social
reformers—United States—Biography—Juvenile literature. I. Title. II. Series.
E185.97.T8K74 2006
306.3'62'092—dc22   2004027195

Summary: An introduction to the life of Sojourner Truth, the former slave who became a
    speaker against slavery.

Editorial Credits
Megan Schoeneberger and Roberta Basel, editors; Juliette Peters, set designer; Patrick D.
    Dentinger, book designer and illustrator; Kelly Garvin, photo researcher/photo editor

Photo Credits
Battle Creek Historical Society, 1, 5, 17 (inset), 23
Corbis/Bettmann, 20–21
Getty Images, Inc./Hulton Archive, cover, 19; Time Life Pictures, 25
Historic Northampton, Northampton, Massachusetts, 15
Library of Congress, 18, 27
Mary Evans Picture Library, 10; The Women's Library, 17
North Wind Picture Archives, 8, 9
Senate House State Historic Site/New York State Office of Parks, Recreation and Historic
    Preservation, 6–7
SuperStock Inc./Superstock, 12–13
U.S. Postal Service, 26

1 2 3 4 5 6 10 09 08 07 06 05

Table of Contents

Chapter 1

Ain't I a Woman?

Sojourner Truth stood like a queen in the front of the room. A former **slave**, Sojourner had never gone to school. She could not read or write. She didn't always speak proper English. But when she spoke with her deep voice, people listened.

It was 1851. Sojourner stood before a women's rights meeting in Akron, Ohio. Some men believed that women were weak and didn't deserve the same rights as men. Sojourner laughed at the idea.

Sojourner held up her right arm. Years of hard work had made her strong. "Look at me," she said. "Ain't I a woman?" She could work as hard as any man. She thought she deserved the same rights.

FREE LECTURE!

SOJOURNER TRUTH,

Who has been a slave in the State of New York, and who has been a Lecturer for the last twenty-three years, whose characteristics have been so vividly portrayed by Mrs. Harriet Beecher Stowe, as the African Sybil, will deliver a lecture upon the present issues of the day,

At   On

And will give her experience as a Slave mother and religious woman. She comes highly recommended as a public speaker, having the approval of many thousands who have heard her earnest appeals, among whom are Wendell Phillips, Wm. Lloyd Garrison, and other distinguished men of the nation.

☞ At the close of her discourse she will offer for sale her photograph and a few of her choice songs.

A poster advertised one of Sojourner's speeches.

When Sojourner finished speaking, the audience clapped loudly. The people were moved by Sojourner's powerful speech.

5

Chapter 2

A Slave Named Isabella

Sojourner Truth began life as a slave named Isabella. She was born sometime around 1797 in a cabin in Rosendale, New York. Nobody wrote down her exact birthday.

Isabella's parents, James and Elizabeth, were slaves. They had 11 children before Isabella. But only Isabella's brother Peter was still with them when she was born. All of their other children had been sold.

Isabella and her family belonged to Johannes Hardenbergh. The Hardenberghs were Dutch. They and their slaves spoke only Dutch.

This painting shows the area in New York where Isabella was born.

A New Master

When Isabella was 3, she and her family became the property of Hardenbergh's son Charles. He moved them into a cold, damp cellar. Isabella and the other slaves slept on hard wooden boards over the muddy floor.

Slave children often worked in fields. ▼

8

Isabella worked hard. She picked vegetables and carried buckets of water. She washed clothes. She helped cook and clean. Isabella worried that she would be sold, like her brothers and sisters had been. She didn't want to be taken from her family.

Bought and Sold

Around 1806, Charles Hardenbergh sold Isabella and Peter in a slave **auction**. One man bought Peter for $100. Another man named John Neely bought Isabella, along with some sheep, for $100.

▲ Children were often sold away from their parents at slave auctions.

▲ Slaves feared being punished by their owners.

The Neelys were not kind to Isabella. They didn't give her shoes to wear. Isabella's half-frozen feet hurt terribly through the cold New York winter. When she couldn't understand their English commands, the Neelys would hit Isabella.

Around 1808, the Neelys sold Isabella to Martinus Schriver, a local fisherman. Isabella helped Schriver fish. She also cooked and cleaned. She gathered herbs and roots from the forest.

A New Family

In 1810, Schriver sold Isabella to a wealthy man, John Dumont. Dumont made Isabella marry one of his slaves, Thomas. Isabella and Thomas had their first baby, Diana, in 1815. Over the next few years, they had four more children named Elizabeth, Hannah, Peter, and Sophia.

FACT!

While working for Schriver, Isabella began to smoke a pipe. Isabella smoked a pipe most of her life.

Chapter 3

Free at Last

In 1824, New York passed a new law. Any slave born before 1799 would be free in 1827. Dumont told Isabella that he would free her in 1826. But Dumont broke his promise. Isabella decided to run away.

One morning, Isabella wrapped some food in a cloth. She took her baby, Sophia. She ran through the woods to the home of the Van Wagenen family.

Dumont soon found Isabella. He demanded her return. The Van Wagenens paid Dumont $25 for Isabella and Sophia. The Van Wagenens then set Isabella and Sophia free.

White people sometimes helped runaway slaves.

Isabella next fought to free her son, Peter. Dumont sold Peter to a family in Alabama. In New York, selling a slave to someone in another state was illegal. The Van Wagenens gave Isabella $5 for a lawyer. In court, the judge freed Peter.

To New York City

In 1828, Isabella and Peter boarded a ship to New York City. Isabella had heard newly freed slaves could find jobs there. Isabella left Sophia with her other children at Dumont's farm. She couldn't take care of a young child while she worked.

Isabella got a job as a maid. For the first time, she earned money for her hard work. She joined a church for African Americans. Isabella and the church members took food and clothing to the poor.

FACT!

When she was first freed, Isabella changed her name. She called herself Isabella Van Wagenen, after the kind family who helped her.

Isabella worked as a
maid to earn money.

Kingdom of God

In 1833, Isabella moved
to Sing Sing, New York. She
joined a religious group
called the "Kingdom of God."
The group's leader was the
Prophet Matthias. He
believed that God was
speaking through him.

In 1834, some church
members accused Matthias
and Isabella of poisoning a
man. Isabella hired a lawyer.
Both she and Matthias were
found not guilty. The judge
ordered the accusers to pay
Isabella $125.

Chapter 4

Call Me Sojourner

In 1843, Isabella had a **vision**. She believed that she saw God, who told her to leave New York and travel west. He wanted Isabella to speak out against what was wrong in the country.

Isabella decided to leave her slave name behind. She changed her name to Sojourner. A **sojourner** is someone who travels from place to place. Isabella chose the last name Truth. She wanted to tell people the truth.

Speaking the Truth

Sojourner left New York on foot. She walked from town to town. She spoke to churches and other groups.

Isabella changed her name to Sojourner Truth in 1843. Her signature is shown in the inset.

Sojourner spoke about ending slavery. Slaves weren't paid for their hard work. They were property, same as a house or a pair of shoes. Sojourner believed it was wrong for someone to own another person.

Sojourner also spoke about women's rights. She wanted women to be able to go to school and get jobs. She also said that women should be able to vote and serve on juries.

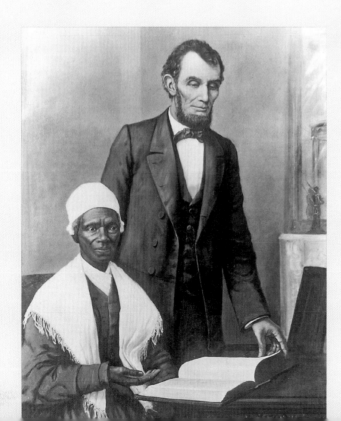

Sojourner visited President Abraham Lincoln in 1864 to talk about ending slavery.

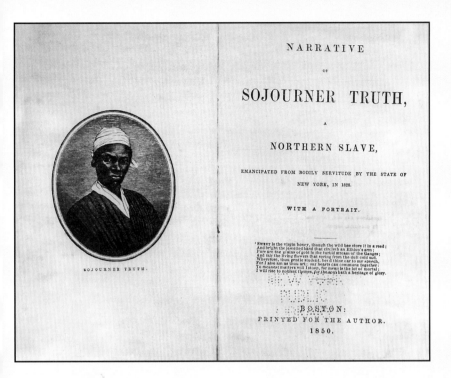

Sojourner's book was printed in 1850.

QUOTE

"I can't read books, but I can read the people."
—Sojourner Truth

In 1850, Sojourner Truth told her life story to her friend Olive Gilbert. Gilbert wrote a book called *The Narrative of Sojourner Truth*. Sojourner sold the book to help pay for her travels.

In 1856, Sojourner visited Battle Creek, Michigan. She decided to buy a house nearby.

Chapter 5

After Slavery

On April 9, 1865, the Civil War (1861–1865) ended. Just a few months later, the government set all slaves free. Sojourner's children and grandchildren were now free.

After the war, most former slaves had no jobs or homes. Sojourner thought the government should give them land in the West. There, she thought, the former slaves could build new lives.

Sojourner visited Kansas, Missouri, Iowa, and Wisconsin to meet with lawmakers. She spoke to people about her idea. Many people signed **petitions** to support the plan. But her idea was not accepted. The government did not give land to the former slaves.

Freed slaves still lived in poor conditions after the Civil War.

QUOTE

"If women want any rights more than they's got, why don't they just take them, and not be talking about it."
—Sojourner Truth

Between 1864 and 1868, Sojourner worked for the National Freedmen's Relief Association and the Freedmen's Bureau. She helped newly freed slaves find jobs and homes.

Fighting for Rights

One day Sojourner and a white friend got on a streetcar. The driver of the car told Sojourner to get off. She didn't listen and went to find a seat. The man tried to push her off the streetcar. She fell against the door and hurt her shoulder.

Sojourner didn't forget about what the man had done. She knew his actions were wrong. Sojourner told the driver's boss, and the man was fired. She then took the man to court for hurting her. She won the case.

Sojourner had strong beliefs about equal rights. ➤

Chapter 6

Shooting Star

Sojourner worked hard until she was very old. When she was 80, she gave a speech to the Michigan State Senate. She told the government leaders that she was against the death **penalty**. She believed a murderer should be put in prison and not killed.

In 1883, Sojourner became ill. She knew that her life was coming to an end. "I'm going home like a shooting star," she told her family. On November 26, Sojourner died. She is buried in Battle Creek, Michigan.

Sojourner posed for this photograph late in her life.

The postage stamp featuring Sojourner showed her giving a speech.

Legacy

Today, Americans honor Sojourner's life. The city of Battle Creek declared May 18 Sojourner Truth Day. In 1981, she was added to the National Women's Hall of Fame. The U.S. Postal Service honored Sojourner with a postage stamp in 1986.

Sojourner was a brave, strong woman. She fought for what she believed in and spoke out against the things she felt were wrong. In her powerful speeches, she told the truth. She inspired many people.

Fast Facts

Full name: Named Isabella at birth; she later changed her name to Sojourner Truth.

Birth: About 1797

Death: November 26, 1883

Hometown: Rosendale, New York

Parents: James and Elizabeth

Siblings: About 11, including Michael, Nancy, Peter, and Sophia

Husband: Thomas

Children: Diana, Elizabeth, Hannah, Peter, and Sophia

Education: No formal education

Time Line

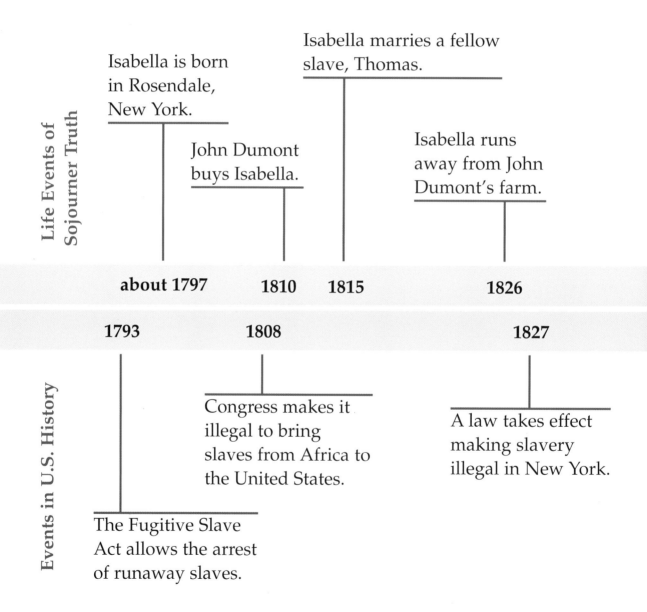

Life Events of Sojourner Truth

Isabella is born in Rosendale, New York.

John Dumont buys Isabella.

Isabella marries a fellow slave, Thomas.

Isabella runs away from John Dumont's farm.

about 1797   1810   1815   1826

1793   1808   1827

Events in U.S. History

The Fugitive Slave Act allows the arrest of runaway slaves.

Congress makes it illegal to bring slaves from Africa to the United States.

A law takes effect making slavery illegal in New York.

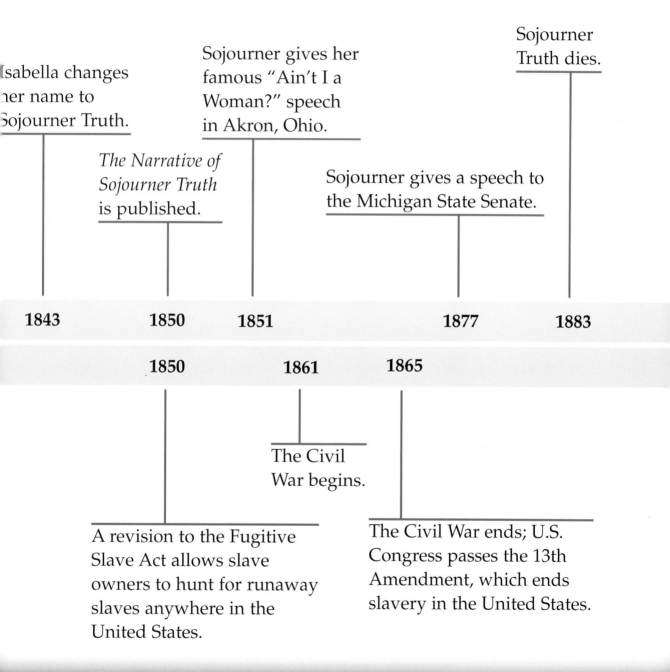

Isabella changes her name to Sojourner Truth.

The Narrative of Sojourner Truth is published.

Sojourner gives her famous "Ain't I a Woman?" speech in Akron, Ohio.

Sojourner gives a speech to the Michigan State Senate.

Sojourner Truth dies.

| 1843 | 1850 | 1851 | 1877 | 1883 |

| 1850 | 1861 | 1865 |

The Civil War begins.

A revision to the Fugitive Slave Act allows slave owners to hunt for runaway slaves anywhere in the United States.

The Civil War ends; U.S. Congress passes the 13th Amendment, which ends slavery in the United States.

Glossary

auction (AWK-shuhn)—a sale where something is sold to the person who offers the most money

penalty (PEN-uhl-tee)—a punishment

petition (puh-TISH-uhn)—a written request signed by many people asking those in power to change their policies or actions

prophet (PROF-it)—a person who claims to be a messenger of God

slave (SLAYV)—a person owned by another person; slaves were not free to choose their homes or jobs.

sojourner (SOH-jurn-uhr)—a person who travels from place to place

vision (VIZH-uhn)—something seen in a dream

Internet Sites

FactHound offers a safe, fun way to find Internet sites related to this book. All of the sites on FactHound have been researched by our staff.

Here's how:

1. Visit *www.facthound.com*
2. Type in this special code **0736843485** for age-appropriate sites. Or enter a search word related to this book for a more general search.
3. Click on the **Fetch It** button.

FactHound will fetch the best sites for you!

Read More

Jaffe, Elizabeth Dana. *Sojourner Truth.* Compass Point Early Biographies. Minneapolis: Compass Point Books, 2001.

Mattern, Joanne. *Sojourner Truth: Early Abolitionist.* Reading Power. New York: PowerKids Press, 2003.

Ruffin, Frances E. *Her Story, Her Words: The Narrative of Sojourner Truth.* Great Moments in American History. New York: Rosen, 2004.

Index